SPORTS
STARTERS

Huddle Up
Football

Bobbie Kalman & John Crossingham

 Crabtree Publishing Company

www.crabtreebooks.com

SPORTS STARTERS

Created by Bobbie Kalman

Dedicated by Michael Hodge
To Matt and Jen. Congratulations on starting your new life together.

Editor-in-Chief
Bobbie Kalman

Writing team
Bobbie Kalman
John Crossingham

Substantive editor
Kelley MacAulay

Project editor
Michael Hodge

Editors
Molly Aloian
Kathryn Smithyman

Photo research
Crystal Foxton

Design
Margaret Amy Salter

Production coordinator
Heather Fitzpatrick

Consultant
Jason Aikens
Collections Curator
Pro Football Hall of Fame

Illustrations
All illustrations by David Calder except:
Bonna Rouse: pages 6-7 (football field)

Photographs
Associated Press: page 13
Icon SMI: page 14; Matt Brown: page 19; Jeff Carlick: page 21; Mark Cowan: pages 24, 28;
    Hans Deryk/Toronto Star/ZUMA Press: page 29; Bob Leverone/TSN/ZUMA Press: page 23;
    James D. Smith: page 20; WD: page 16
iStockphoto.com: James Boulette: pages 4, 10-11; Sean Locke: page 27; Curtis J. Morley: page 8;
    Todd Taulman: page 3; Tony Tremblay: page 31
© Photosport.com: pages 12, 15, 17, 18, 22, 25, 26
© ShutterStock.com/G. Lewis: page 30
Other images by Digital Stock and Photodisc

Library and Archives Canada Cataloguing in Publication

Kalman, Bobbie, 1947-
    Huddle up football / Bobbie Kalman & John Crossingham.

(Sports starters)
Includes index.
ISBN 978-0-7787-3137-5 (bound)
ISBN 978-0-7787-3169-6 (pbk.)

    1. Football--Juvenile literature. I. Crossingham, John, 1974- II. Title.
III. Series: Sports starters (St. Catharines, Ont.)

GV950.7.K34 2007   j796.332   C2007-900945-X

Library of Congress Cataloging-in-Publication Data

Kalman, Bobbie.
    Huddle up football / Bobbie Kalman & John Crossingham.
        p. cm. -- (Sports starters)
    Includes index.
    ISBN-13: 978-0-7787-3137-5 (rlb)
    ISBN-10: 0-7787-3137-5 (rlb)
    ISBN-13: 978-0-7787-3169-6 (pb)
    ISBN-10: 0-7787-3169-3 (pb)
    1. Football--Juvenile literature. I. Crossingham, John, 1974- II. Title.
III. Series.

GV950.7.K27 2007
796.332--dc22
                                        2007005077

Crabtree Publishing Company

www.crabtreebooks.com   1-800-387-7650

Published in Canada
Crabtree Publishing
616 Welland Ave.
St. Catharines, ON
L2M 5V6

Published in the United States
Crabtree Publishing
PMB16A
350 Fifth Ave., Suite 3308
New York, NY 10118

Published in the United Kingdom
Crabtree Publishing
White Cross Mills
High Town, Lancaster
LA1 4XS

Published in Australia
Crabtree Publishing
386 Mt. Alexander Rd.
Ascot Vale (Melbourne)
VIC 3032

Contents

What is football?

Football is North America's most popular **team sport**. In a team sport, two teams play against each other. Football teams play on a large area called a **football field**. Each team tries to score points. A team scores points by carrying or kicking a ball into the other team's **end zone**. The end zone is an area at each end of the field. The team with the most points at the end of the game is the winner.

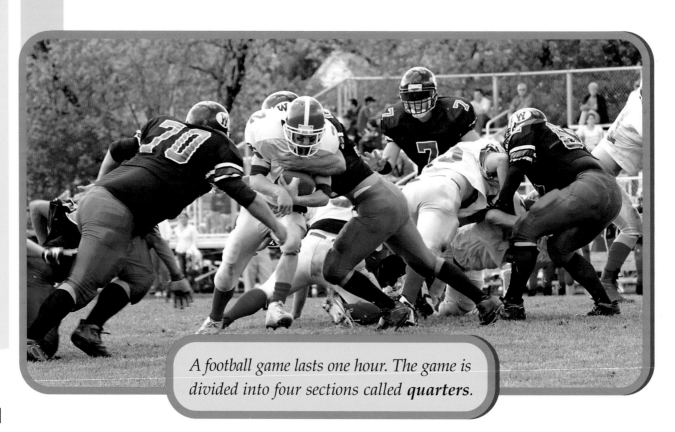

*A football game lasts one hour. The game is divided into four sections called **quarters**.*

Offense or defense?

When a team has the ball, they are **on offense**. The team on offense is trying to score points. The team without the ball is **on defense**. This team is trying to stop its **opponents** from scoring.

A lot of players!

Every football team has a group of players called the **offensive players**. When a team is on offense, its offensive players are on the field. Each team also has a group of players called the **defensive players**. When a team is on defense, its defensive players are on the field.

Each team has eleven players on the field at a time.

On the field

A football field is 120 yards (110 m) long. There are lines called **yard lines** on the field. Yard lines measure the length of the field. **Sidelines** mark the sides of the field. If the ball goes over a sideline, it is **out-of-bounds**. Play stops when the ball is out-of-bounds.

End zones

There is an end zone at both ends of the field. A line called a **goal line** marks the beginning of an end zone. A team scores a **touchdown** by getting the ball into its opponent's end zone. A touchdown is worth six points. A team scores a **field goal** by kicking the ball through its opponent's **goal post**. A field goal is worth three points.

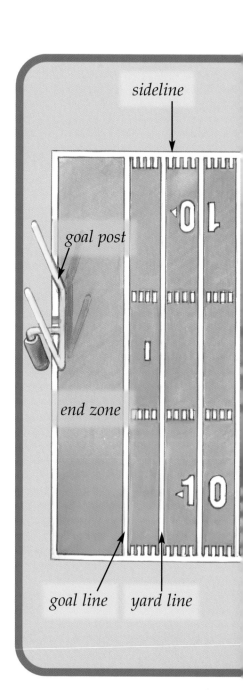

sideline

goal post

end zone

goal line   yard line

On offense

Every football player has a **position**. The offensive positions are shown below in blue. Five players make up a group called the **offensive linemen**. From left to right, the offensive linemen are the **left offensive tackle**, **left guard**, **center**, **right guard**, and **right offensive tackle**. The **tight end** sometimes acts as a sixth offensive lineman.

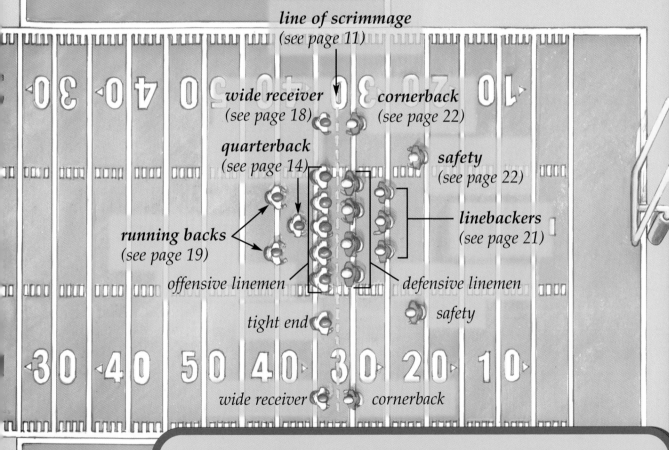

line of scrimmage
(see page 11)

wide receiver
(see page 18)

cornerback
(see page 22)

quarterback
(see page 14)

safety
(see page 22)

running backs
(see page 19)

linebackers
(see page 21)

offensive linemen

defensive linemen

tight end

safety

wide receiver

cornerback

On defense

The defensive positions are shown above in red. The **defensive tackles** and **defensive ends** make up a group of defensive players called the **defensive linemen**.

Kickoff!

Every football team has a group of players called the **special teams**. The special teams are on the field at the start of a football game. The game begins with a **kickoff**. During the kickoff, a player from one team kicks the ball toward players on the other team. A player from the other team catches the ball. He runs with it as far as possible toward his opponent's goal line.

*The player on the right is a **kicker**. He is kicking the ball to the other team.*

Tackled!

As the player runs with the ball, his opponents try to stop him. They stop him by **tackling** him. Tackling means forcing a player to the ground. The yard line where the player hits the ground is where the **first down** begins (see page 10). After the kickoff, the special teams leave the field. The offensive players and the defensive players go out onto the field.

The player with the ball is being tackled.

Four downs

The offensive players have four chances to move the ball toward the other team's end zone. They move the ball by running with it or **passing** it. Each chance to move the ball is called a **down**. The four downs are called first down, **second down**, **third down**, and **fourth down**.

Getting extra downs

The offensive team must move the ball at least ten yards within their four downs. If they move the ball at least ten yards, they get four new downs. Extra downs give the team chances to move the ball even closer to the other team's end zone. The defensive players tackle the offensive players to try to stop them from moving the ball ten yards. If the offensive team doesn't move the ball at least ten yards within four downs, the other team gets the ball.

Drawing the line

The yard line where a down begins is called the **line of scrimmage**. The line of scrimmage is the yard line where the offensive player who is carrying the ball is tackled. The line of scrimmage moves for every down. For example, the spot where the player shown above in blue is tackled will become the new line of scrimmage. The next down will start at this spot.

Kick it!

The offensive players sometimes use their fourth down to kick a field goal. To kick a field goal, the kicker kicks the ball toward the opponent's goal post. If the ball goes through the goal post, the team earns three points. It is hard to kick the ball through the goal post, so the kicker kicks a field goal only if the the team is close to the goal post.

The player on the left is a kicker.
She is kicking a field goal.

Punt it!

Sometimes, the offensive team is too far away from the goal post to score a field goal. Instead, the team will use its fourth down to **punt**. When an offensive team punts, an offensive player called the **punter** kicks the ball down the field, away from his end zone. A player on the defensive team catches the ball and runs with it until he is tackled.

Farther away

The place where the player is tackled becomes the line of scrimmage. The line of scrimmage is farther from the end zone than it would have been if the offensive team had not punted.

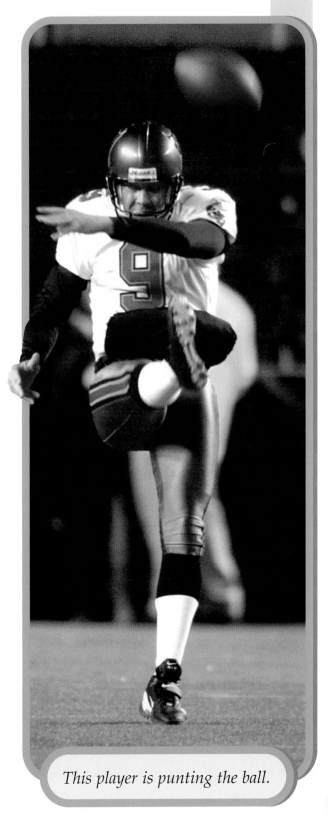

This player is punting the ball.

Quarterbacks

The quarterback leads a team's offensive players. At the beginning of each down, the center **snaps** the ball to the quarterback. The quarterback then gets the ball to a **ball carrier**. The ball carriers are the players who run with the ball toward their opponent's end zone to try to score.

quarterback

During the snap, the center passes the ball through his legs to the quarterback. The quarterback then gets the ball to a ball carrier.

Huddle up!

Before every down, the offensive players have a quick meeting. The meeting is called a **huddle**. During the huddle, the quarterback tells the players which **play** to use. A play is a plan. The play tells each player what she should do during the down. The play helps the ball carriers get past the defensive players and into the end zone.

This team is having a huddle. The quarterback is telling her teammates which play to use.

Offensive linemen

Offensive linemen are the heaviest, strongest offensive players. They begin every down crouched along the line of scrimmage. Offensive linemen do not carry the ball. After the snap, they use their size and strength to stop opponents from tackling the quarterback.

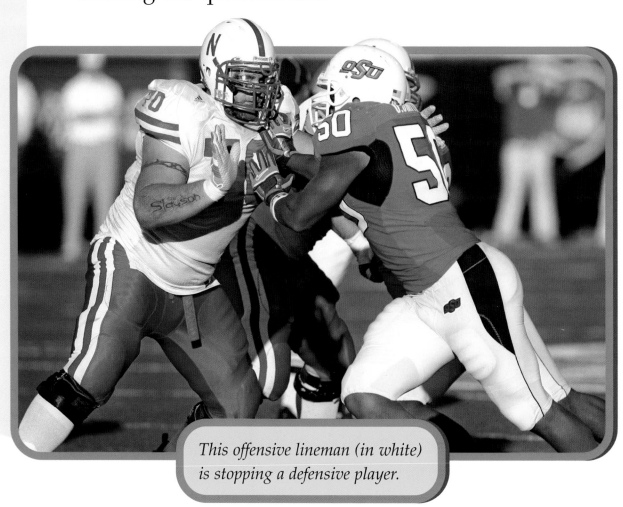

This offensive lineman (in white) is stopping a defensive player.

Protecting the quarterback

To stop opponents from tackling the quarterback, offensive linemen **block** them. An offensive lineman blocks a defensive player by pushing the player away from the quarterback. Offensive linemen block defensive players so that the quarterback has time to get the ball to a ball carrier.

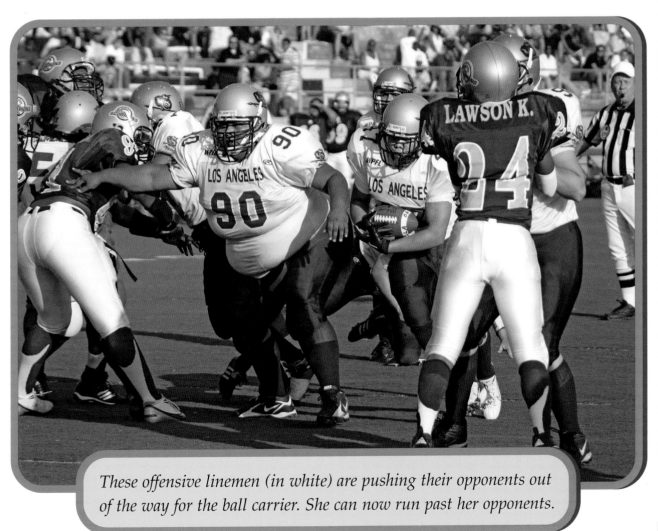

These offensive linemen (in white) are pushing their opponents out of the way for the ball carrier. She can now run past her opponents.

Ball carriers

This wide receiver has caught the ball. She will now try to make it to the end zone to score.

The wide receivers and running backs are the offensive team's main ball carriers. After the snap, the wide receivers run down the field toward the end zone. The quarterback gets the ball to the wide receivers by passing.

Tight catches

The tight end sometimes plays as a third wide receiver. Tight ends stay closer to the line of scrimmage than where wide receivers stay. They catch shorter passes than wide receivers do.

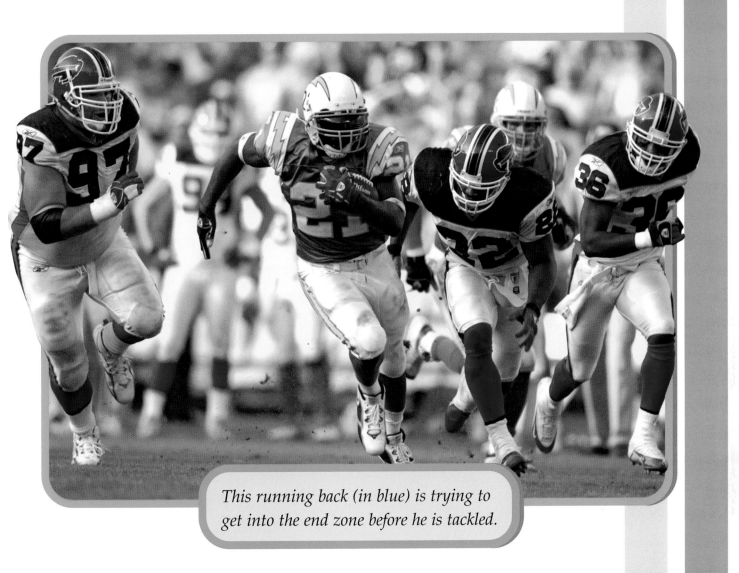

This running back (in blue) is trying to get into the end zone before he is tackled.

On the run

Sometimes the quarterback hands the ball to a running back instead of passing it to a wide receiver. Handing the ball to a player is called a **handoff**. During a handoff, the quarterback holds out the ball, and the running back takes it and runs. Once he has the ball, the running back runs toward the end zone.

The front seven

The **front seven** is a group of defensive linemen and linebackers. The defensive linemen are two defensive tackles and two defensive ends. The defensive linemen start every down crouched along the line of scrimmage. They face the offensive linemen. The defensive linemen are strong and heavy. They try to push past the offensive linemen. If they get past, they tackle the quarterback if he has the ball.

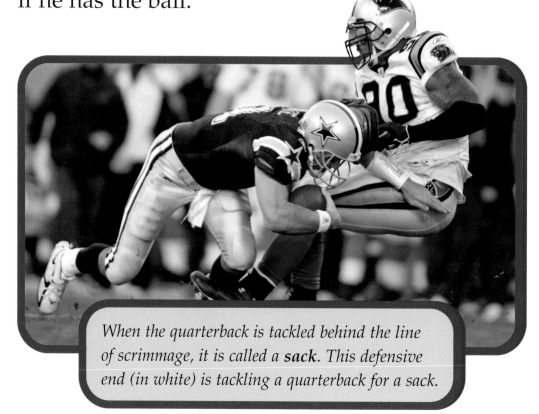

*When the quarterback is tackled behind the line of scrimmage, it is called a **sack**. This defensive end (in white) is tackling a quarterback for a sack.*

The linebackers

Before the snap, the linebackers stand behind the defensive linemen. After the snap, a linebacker's job is to tackle whoever has the ball. A linebacker may tackle a running back or a wide receiver.

If the quarterback has handed the ball to a running back, the linebackers tackle the running back. This linebacker (in white) is tackling a running back.

The secondary

The **secondary** is a group of four defensive players. It includes two cornerbacks and two safeties. Each cornerback **covers** one wide receiver. To cover a player is to try to prevent her from catching a pass. If a wide receiver catches a pass, a cornerback tackles her.

Safeties

The safeties are extra defensive players. They go wherever help is needed most. For example, the safeties often help a cornerback cover the other team's best wide receiver.

The cornerback is shown above in red. She has stopped the pass from reaching a wide receiver.

Interception!

The secondary often tries to catch the offensive team's passes. When a defensive player catches an opponent's pass, it is called an **interception**. A player who makes an interception can run toward the opponent's end zone and try to score a touchdown!

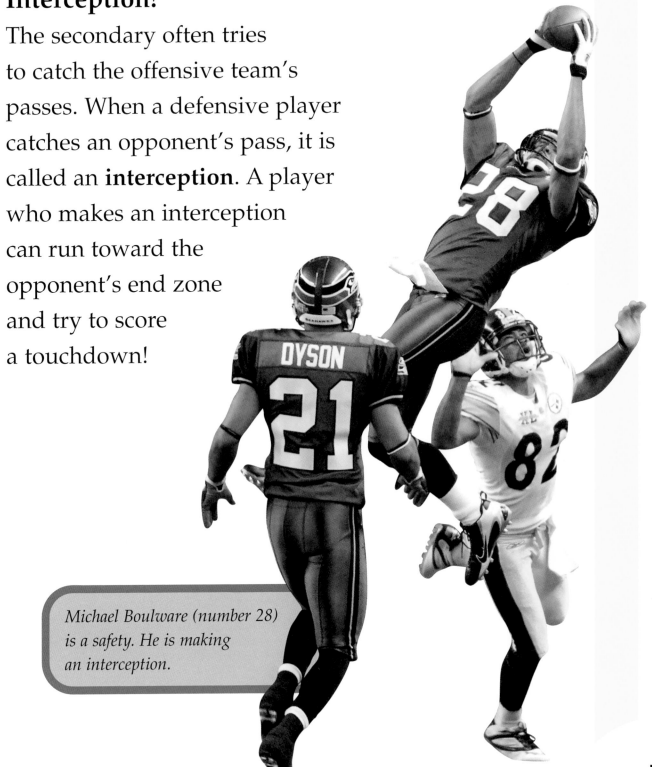

Michael Boulware (number 28) is a safety. He is making an interception.

Special teams

During kickoffs, punts, and field goals, each team's special teams players come onto the field. Special teams often include a kicker or a punter. The kicker and punter are the only players who kick the ball.

During a punt, the center snaps the ball to the punter. The punter then punts the ball as far down the field as possible.

Extra points

After a player scores a touchdown, her team is allowed to attempt an **extra point**. The special teams players come onto the field for the extra point. To kick an extra point, the kicker aims the ball at the other team's goal post. If the ball goes through the goal post, the kicker earns one point for her team.

This kicker is kicking an extra point for her team.

Follow the rules

There are seven **officials** in a football game. The officials make sure the players follow the rules. Teams sometimes disagree with an official's **call**, or decision about whether they followed the rules. At these times, the official who made the call speaks with the other officials to get their opinions. Checking with the other officials helps make sure that the right call is made.

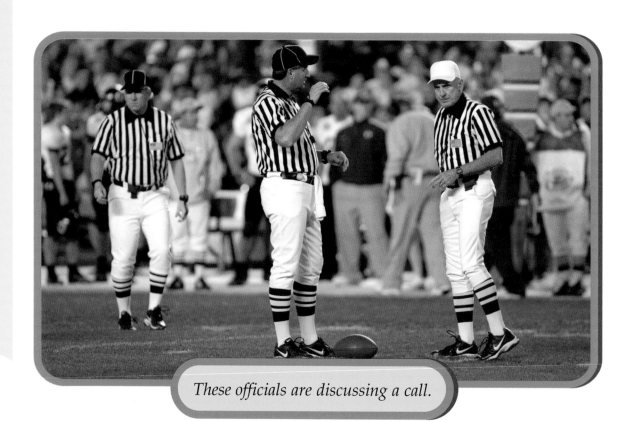

These officials are discussing a call.

Pay the price

When a player breaks the rules, his or her team is given a **penalty**. For example, if a defensive player holds on to an opponent who does not have the ball, the defensive player's team gets a penalty. This penalty is called **holding**. When the defensive team gets a penalty, the offensive team **gains yards**, or gets to move closer to its opponent's end zone. If the offensive team gets a penalty, however, it **loses yards**, or has to move farther away from its opponent's end zone.

penalty flag

*When an official sees a penalty, he tosses a **penalty flag** onto the field.*

Football leagues

The **National Football League**, or **NFL**, is the world's best-known football **league**. A league is a group of teams that play against one another. The NFL has 32 teams from cities across the United States. The NFL is a **professional league**. In a professional league, players get paid to play a sport.

The Super Bowl
The NFL's **championship game** is called the **Super Bowl**. The Super Bowl happens every year in February. Tom Brady, shown above, is the quarterback for the New England Patriots. He has led the team to three Super Bowl wins.

The NCAA

The **National Collegiate Athletic Association**, or **NCAA**, is a league for college players. College football games are very popular events in the United States. Many great college players become players in the NFL.

The CFL

The **Canadian Football League**, or **CFL**, is Canada's professional football league. Canadian football is played on a larger field than the American football field. The teams also have only three downs at a time instead of four. The CFL championship game is called the **Grey Cup**. Damon Allen, shown right, plays in the CFL. He is one of the best quarterbacks in history.

Now it's your turn!

If you are interested in playing football, you can probably get started right away. Joining a youth league, such as **Pop Warner**, is a great way to make new friends and learn to play.

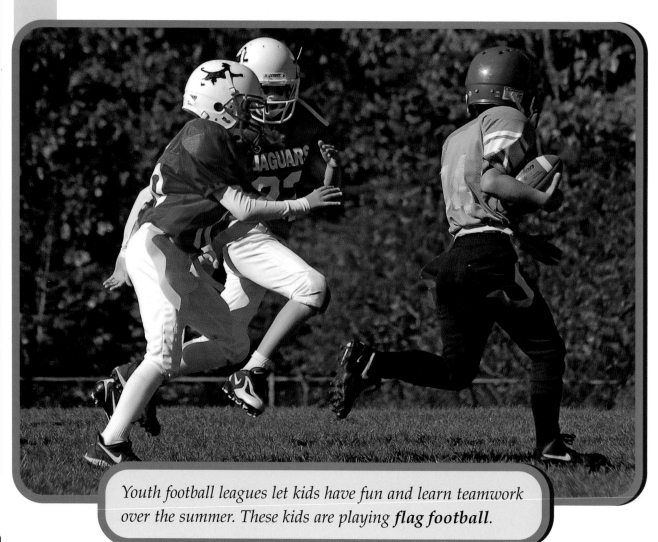

*Youth football leagues let kids have fun and learn teamwork over the summer. These kids are playing **flag football**.*

Team spirit, school spirit

Many schools have football teams. These teams usually have a lot of fans at the school. Joining a school team is a great way to learn the sport. Cheering for the team is also a lot of fun!

These kids are having fun playing football.

Glossary

Note: Boldfaced words that are defined in the text may not appear in the glossary.

championship game A game played to determine who is the best team

defensive ends The two players on the outside of the defensive line

defensive tackles The two players on the inside of the defensive line

field goal A kick toward the opponent's goal post; if the ball goes through the goal post, the team earns three points

flag football A kind of football in which there is no tackling; instead, a player must take a flag from the opponent who has the ball

kicker The offensive player who kicks field goals, kickoffs, and extra points

opponent A player on another team

out-of-bounds Describing a ball that has gone over a sideline

position The area of the field in which a player does his or her job

punter The offensive player who punts the ball

snap The action of the center passing the ball through his or her legs to the quarterback

special teams A group of eleven players that plays during kicks

tackle The action of bringing an opponent to the ground

touchdown A score in which a player carries the ball into the opponent's end zone or catches the ball in the opponent's end zone

Index

Printed in the U.S.A.